THREE HIGHWAYS OF THE COLONIES

Proceedings of the Scituate Historical Society

By Harvey H. Pratt

ISBN: 978-0-9910923-3-8

Digitally Reproduced in 2015 by:

CONVERPAGE
23 Acorn Street
Scituate, MA 02066
781-378-1996

BOSTON

BOSTON BAY

N.

W. E.

S.

MILTON

QUINCY

3 4
5 6

8

BRAINTREE

WEYMOUTH

Plymouth & Bay

ROAD

9

HINGHAM CENTRE

HINGHAM

COHASSET

10

THE COUNTRY WAY

SCITUATE

12

13

HOLBROOK

NORWELL

MARSHFIELD

ROCKLAND HANOVER

MASSACHUSETTS PATH

14

HANSON

PEMBROKE

15

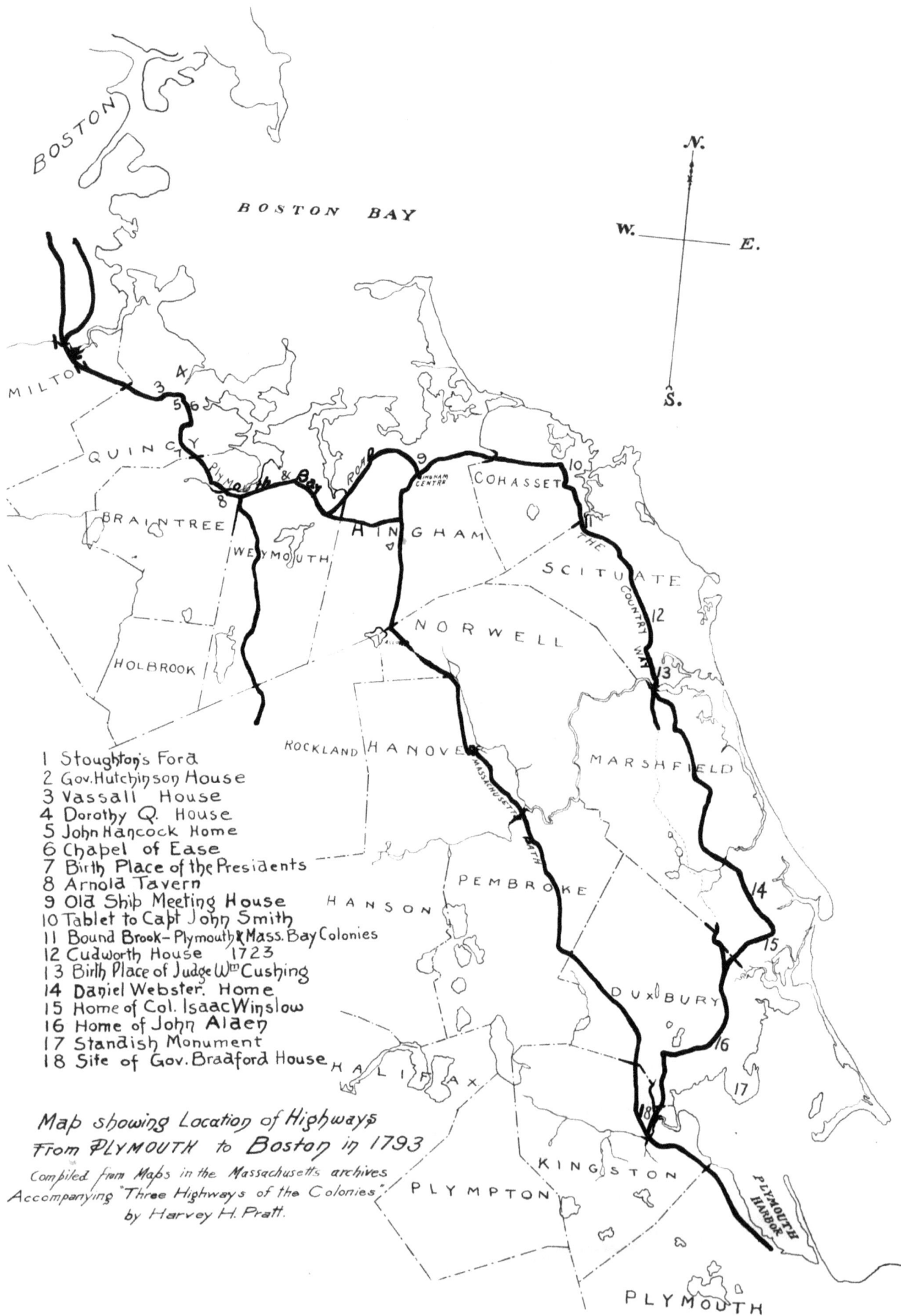

1 Stoughton's Ford
2 Gov. Hutchinson House
3 Vassall House
4 Dorothy Q. House
5 John Hancock Home
6 Chapel of Ease
7 Birth Place of the Presidents
8 Arnold Tavern
9 Old Ship Meeting House
10 Tablet to Capt John Smith
11 Bound Brook – Plymouth & Mass. Bay Colonies
12 Cudworth House 1723
13 Birth Place of Judge Wm Cushing
14 Daniel Webster. Home
15 Home of Col. Isaac Winslow
16 Home of John Alden
17 Standish Monument
18 Site of Gov. Bradford House

DUXBURY

16

17

18

HALIFAX

Map showing Location of Highways
From PLYMOUTH to Boston in 1793

Compiled from Maps in the Massachusetts archives
Accompanying "Three Highways of the Colonies"
by Harvey H. Pratt.

PLYMPTON

KINGSTON

PLYMOUTH HARBOR

PLYMOUTH

COCKAYNE, BOSTON

THREE HIGHWAYS OF THE COLONIES

By HARVEY H. PRATT

When Phineas Pratt undertook his perilous journey from Wessagusset to inform the Plymouth colonists of the attack contemplated by Squanto's[1] Indians in further reprisal for the depredations of Weston's colonists, there was neither path nor blazed trail to point the way between the locations where the two bands of adverturesome men had each established its habitat. Mr. Governor, Mr. Deputy, Sir Richard Saltonstall, Mr. Vassall and their associates had not then sought the patent from King Charles which eight years later became the corner stone for the erection by Governor Winthrop of the "Great Colony." Such intercourse as had occurred between the Pilgrims and the "rude and prophane fellows,"[2] who were Weston's colonizers at Wessagusset, was accomplished by water in the ungainly shallops with which each was provided. Pratt in his narrative tells of his early suspicions of the Indians and the designs by them upon the lives of his own comrades and the men at Plymouth. It was March, 1623. Misleading the "Salvages" as to his purpose, he managed to get away from their vicinity and started through the woods for Plymouth with neither compass or guide; and for sustenance, a small quantity of parched corn and a few "ground nutts."

"Then looking roundabout me (goes the narrative) I ran southward till three of the clock, but the snow being in many places I was more distressed because of my footsteps. The sun being beclouded, I wandered not knowing my way; but at the going down of the sun it appeared red. Then hearing a great howling of wolves, I came to a river. Then water being deep and cold and many rocks, I passed through with much ado.

[1]They were Squanto's tribesmen. The chief himself had been stricken and died at Chatham while with Governor Bradford on an expedition seeking trade with the Indians at that place

[2]Weston himself so describes them. Young's Chronicles of the Pilgrims, page 296—note.

1

Then I was in great distress—faint for want of food, weary with running, fearing to make a fire because of them that pursued me. Then I came to a deep dell or hole, there being much wood fallen into it. Then I said in my thoughts, this is God's Providence that here I may make a fire. Then having made a fire the stars began to appear and I saw Ursa Major and the * * * * [1] pole yet fearing * * * * beclouded. The day following I began to travel * * * * but being unable, I went back to the fire the day foll * * * * sun shined and about three of the clock I came to that part * * * * Plymouth bay where there is a town of later time * * * * Duxbury. Then passing by the water on my left hand * * * * came to a brook and there was a path. Having but a short time to consider * * * * fearing to go beyond the plantation, I kept running in the path; then passing through James River[2] I said in my thoughts, now I am as a deer chased * * * * the wolves. If I perish what will be the condit * * * * of distressed Englishmen. Then finding a peice of a* * * * I took it up and carried it in my hand. Then finding a * * * * of a jurkin. I carried them under my arm. Then I said in my * * * * God hath given me these two tokens for my comfort, that now he will give me my life for a pray * * * *. Then running down the hill I * * * * an Englishman coming in the path before me. Then I sat down on a tree and rising up to salute him said:

"Mr. Hamden[3] I am glad to see you alive." He said, I am glad and full of wonder to see you alive, let us sit down, I see you are weary. I said "Let us * * * * * eat some parched corn." Then he said I know the caus * * * * com * * * * Massasoit hath sent word to the Governor to let him * * * * that Aberdikies and his confederates have contrived a plot hoping * * * * all English people in one day here."

Thus began a community of interest in the common defence which in later years welded together Puritan and Pilgrim—colonizer and religious enthusiast—two forces which brought into being the patriot who threw

[1]This excerpt from Phineas Pratt's narrative is made from the printed copy of the original manuscript published by the Massachusetts Historical Society in 1858. Mass. Hist. Soc. Coll. Fourth Series Vol IV, Page 474. The manuscript "Is torn at the edges and portions of the writing are obliterated. A portion also is lost. In this form it was presented to the General Court of the Colony of Massachusetts Bay in 1662." No attempt has been made here either to follow the original in its quaint spelling or supply its missing parts.

[2]Jones' River between Kingston and Plymouth.

[3]It has been claimed that this gentleman was John Hampden the great English patriot who is said to have come with Weston's colonizers in the Charity and to have met Pratt at Monhegan or Weymouth. Alexander Young, the editor of Winslow's Good News, a most careful and learned historian, puts up most convincing proof to the contrary. Young's Chronicles of the Pilgrims, Page 314—note.

off the domination of a crown and erected a secure and lasting commonwealth.

With the failure of Weston's project at Weymouth and that of Morton's Episcopaleans at Merrymount there was no occasion for the Pilgrims to go into either place except as fishing or other expeditions took them by sea.

Local ways and lanes were of course laid out and established in the town of Plymouth during the first years of the settlement; but no attempt was made to extend them beyond the town limits until 1634, when the Governor and Assistants:—

"Apoynted for laying out highwayes for Duxbyside, Capt. Miles Standish, Mr. William Collier, Jonathan Brewster, William Palmer, Steven Trace.

For Plymouth. John Jeney, Fra: Cooke, Manaseh Kempton, Ed Bangs, Nicholas Snow, John Winslowe, James Hurst."

At a similar court held three years later a jury consisting of Plymouth and Duxbury men to the number of twelve, laid out the road:—

"From the towne of Plymouth to Joanes River, as it was cleared provided it be holpen at Mr. Allerton's by going through the old cowe yard * * * * at the river, the place being comonly called the Old Wading Place, and so through a valley up the hill, and then to turne straight to Abraham Pierces ground, and through his ground as it is marked, and so the old path to Massechusett, leaving Mr. Bradford's house upon the west."

"Also we allowe a heigh way from the cutt betweene William Bassett and Francis Sprage, to goe to Ducksborrow towne; the heighway to be continued from William Bassets garden or orchard, through John Washburnes ground to William Palmers gate, as it now is, and so along through Peeter Browne ground by the outeside of which we allow a way to the marsh, and up to the woods; the way still to passe by Henry Howland's house leaving it upon the east side, so keeping the old way through the marsh to Mr. Alden's house, and from thence through a valley which leadeth to the corner of Phillip Delaney's field so to pass Edward Bumpas house, and fourty foote to be allowed above his house straight to Rowland Leghornes house, and so passinge above the house to Greenes Harbor path[1]."

[1]Plymouth Colony Records, Vol. I, page 58. The "Old Path to Massachusetts" lead to the colony of Massachusetts Bay. "Mr. Bradford's house" was that of Governor Bradford; Mr. Alden's house, "on the way to goe to Ducksborrow" was the residence of John Alden and "Greenes Harbor path" was the way to Marshfield.

3

This was the beginning of "The Country Way" as the shore road from Plymouth to the "Bay Colony," passing through Duxbury, Marshfield, Scituate, Cohasset and Hingham, was called; and of the inland route, "The Massachusetts Path," sometimes erroneously called the "King's Highway," but later known as "Queen Anne's Turnpike" traversing Kingston, Duxbury, Hanover and Hingham—the two arteries of communication between the Pilgrim and Puritan communities. They converged in Hingham, and thus joined, continued on to the northward by the Old Ship Meeting House, through old Braintree and Dorchester, where it was known as the "Plymouth and Bay Road," to Boston.

There was at first little intercolonial use for either. It was not until 1643 when the confederation of the four colonies, known as the United Colonies of New England, for their better protection against the Indians, was consummated, that a regular use was made of them. At first, it is probable that the shore road "The Country Way" was the one used. The early commissioners from Plymouth were John Brown of Plymouth, Edward Winslow of Marshfield, William Collier of Duxbury and Timothy Hatherly of Scituate. It is certain that the three last named would seek the most direct course to their destination in journeying to the place of the performance of their duties. This was "The Country Way." The three commissioners traveled together with a guard and upon horseback.

This belief that they proceeded by way of the shore towns and not through the "Massachusetts Path," is strengthened by an incident which occurred in Scituate in 1655.

Isaac Buck, blacksmith at that place and ensign of The Train Band, had aspired to become a sargeant of the company. He was a good politician as well as a good soldier and succeeded in having himself chosen to the coveted position by his comrades in arms. This was against the slate previously prepared by the Governor and Assistants of whom John Browne of Plymouth,

Commissioner of the United Colonies, was one. The record of what subsequently took place tells the story of the trouble:—

"Whereas there is a complaint brought to us of the unworthy carriages of some persons in the traine band of Scittuate in the choise of their sargeants, which doth seem to us to be in contempt of the government, in that they voted for divers unmeet persons for such a place, and alsoe in voteing for the ensigns to bee a sargeant that was formerly assigned to the place by us; now these are therefore to require you that in due time you come together, and make choise of such as are fitt for the place of sargeants, and those men formerly chosen to attend the daise of training and bearing armes as before; and if you give us occation by like complaint, wee shall take further as wee shall see meet.

And wheras wee are informed that Isacke Bucke, the now clark of the said band, on youer last daie of training, when hee called the companie together, did unworthyly misdemean himselfe, wee require him that hee make a publicke acknowledgment therof att the head of the companie the next training day, or otherwise wee hereby require him to make his personal appierance at the General Court to be held for this government the first Tuesday in March next, to answare for his said misdemeanor."

When Brown travelled to the performance of his duties as Commissioner of the United Colonies at New Haven, he must have passed over the Country Way through Scituate to accompany James Cudworth of that town who was also a member of the body. He applied to Buck to shoe his horses. The latter smarting under Brown's action in defeating him for sargeant refused, and for this additional insubordination was subsequently fined twenty shillings.

Although called highways, neither route merited that distinction. The roads were laid out so as to follow the course of least resistance—avoiding marsh lands and boulders, the gates, bars and pallisadoes of land owners and large growths of timber. Along the shore line this latter was less of an obstacle than by the Massachusetts Path. The growth by the sea was of stunted pines and cedars; that inland, larger and of the harder woods. There were six rivers, Jones river in Kingston, the South and North rivers in Marshfield, the Fore and Back rivers in Weymouth and the Neponset in Dorchester, and innumerable brooks to be ferried, forded or swum. On the second day of March, 1636, (Old Style) the Plymouth Colony Court ordered:—

"That Joseph Rogers be allowed a constant ferry over Jones River, neer his dwelling house, and to take a penny for the transportation of each person, he the said Joseph, maintayning a sufficient ferry at that price."

While the ferry may have been sufficient, the price was not; and after two years he abandoned it to George Moore. The passengers were few, and Moore after a six months' effort, resigned his post and moved to Scituate where he later died a pauper. The Court seeing the necessity for transportation at this place thereupon induced John Barker for a grant of forty acres of land adjoining that of former ferryman Rogers, and a two pence fee per person, to become the ferryman and he collected this toll until 1639 when a bridge "passable for a horse and man and cart to goe over" was built and three men each from Plymouth and Duxbury were chosen to assess the cost thereof upon the two towns.

At this time there were three ways across Jones' River, "the wading place," the "stepping stones" and the ferry above described near its mouth. The bridge built there in 1639 was in the line of the Massachusetts Path. Prior to 1685 a bridge was built at the "steping stones" to be maintained by Plymouth and other towns. On July 6, 1685, the town having been indicted for not keeping this bridge in repair:—

"Then also the town chose Major Bradford and Joseph Warren to be their agents at Court to answer the town's presentment relating to Jones River bridge, and to act in the town's behalf with the agents of the four other towns who are ingaged with this town to repair said bridge, for its reparation."[1]

"In 1708 a bridge was ordered to be built where the present bridge stands, and the highway was laid out

[1]Plymouth Town Records July 6, 1685.

6

to cross it. At the same time the old bridge at the "wading place" was ordered to be taken down. It was repaired, however, and the new bridge was not built to take its place until about 1715.[1] About that time the bridge at the "stepping stones" was burned and it was never rebuilt."[2]

In 1638 William Vassall having been granted two hundred acres of land along the North river in Scituate, was obliged in connection with the grant to maintain a ferry to transport man and beast, for which service he might charge not in excess of one penny for a man, four pence for a horse and the same sum for a horse and its rider. He was likewise obliged "to make the way passable for man & beaste through the marshes on both sides of the river at his own Charges."

Farther up the river, where is now the junction of Pembroke and Hanover, William Barstow covenanted with the Plymouth Colony Court Oct. 6, 1656, to build a bridge:—

"By the place wher now passengers go frequently over, the said bridge to bee made sufficient for horse and foot; and he is to lay out and clear and marke a way from the said bridge towards the bay as far as Hughes Crosse, and to open and cleare and marke a way along beyond Hughes Crosse towards the bay, soe as to avoid a certain rocky hill and swamp; and for the true performance of all said particulars, the said William Barstow is to be paid by the Treasurer in the behalf of the countrey the summe of twelve pounds in currant countrey pay."

Nor was this amount the only emolument which Barstow received. Six months after the bridge had been built it was ordered that:—

"William Barstow is allowed by the Court to draw and sell wine, beer, and stronge waters for passengers that come and goe over the bridge he hath lately made, or others that shall have occasion, unless just exception shall come in against him."

Governor Winthrop in his journal speaks of this Hughes' Cross in recounting the incidents of his return trip to Boston after a visit to Plymouth in

[1]Province Laws, Vol. IX, pages 46 and 60; Plymouth Town Records, Vol. II, pages 140, 142, 145.
[2]Plymouth Town Records, Vol. II, page 15. Note.

1632.   The entry has found a frequent place in colonial chronicles and has heretofore been referred to and explained by the writer[1] of this mon'ograph. It is however, by reason of the explanation, worthy of repetition here.

"About five in the morning (says the Journal) the Governor and his company came out of Plymouth; the Governor of Plymouth with the pastor and elder &c accompany them nearly half a mile out of town in the dark. The Lieut. Holmes with two others and the governor's mare came along with them to the great swamp about ten miles. When they came to the great river, they were carried over by one Luddam their guide (as they had been when they came, the stream being very strong and up to the crotch) so the governor called that place Luddam's Ford. Thence they came to a place called Hue's Cross. The Governor being displeased at the name, in respect that such things might hereafter give the Papists occasion the say that their religion was first planted in these parts, changed the name and called it Hue's Folly."

Governor Winthrop was mistaken. The place was called "Hewes Cross Brook."   It took its name from the facts that here the First Herring Brook crossed a small brook and John Hewes a Welchman[2] lived nearby. Winthrop's editor, Savage, calls the Governor's error a "slight usurpation" in that he was not in his own territory. Both he and the Massachusetts Executive however missed the point.

There was a ferry between Weymouth and Morton's Mt. Wollaston before 1639. It crossed the Weymouth Fore River near the site of the present bridge. A road from thence to Dorchester had been "ordered the same year" although it was not laid out until nine years later. Through the means of the ferry it connected with the trail even then called the Countrey Way to Plymouth, passed by the first church of old Braintree, the Chapel of Ease of John Wheelwright the friend of Cromwell, crossed Town River and extended on toward Dorchester.

[1]Pratt—The Early Planters of Scituate.
[2]Deans—History of Scituate, Page 160.
[2]Massachusetts Bay records, Vol. I, Page 280.

At Neponset River was another ferry. In April 1634, Israel Stoughton had been granted liberty to build "a myll, a ware and a bridge over Naponsett Ryver,"[1] and in the following September, he was given the sole privilege on condition that he "shall, make & keepe in repair a sufficient horse bridge over said ryver & shall always from tyme to tyme sell the aylwives he takes there at V. s. per thousand."

If the mill and herring weir prospered the bridge did not, perhaps from the restrictive price put upon the fish. Five years after this concession a license to set up a house and keep a ferry farther up the river from Stoughton's bridge was granted to Bray Wilkins, who however could charge but a penny a person and was obliged, like all of the ferrymen, to carry the magistrates free.

Wilkins found his penny a person as inadequate compensation as did Rogers at Jones River in Kingston. The employment was twice abandoned, and in 1648, this record[2] appears:—

"Uppon certayne information given to this Court, that there is no ferrie keept over Neponsit River between Dorchester & Braintry whereby all that are to passe that way are enforced to head the river, to the great prejudice of those towns thereabouts, & that there yet appeares no man that will keep it unles he may be accommodated with house, land & a bout, at the charge of the Country, its therefore ordered by the authoritie of this Court that Mr. John Glover shall and hath full power given him, either to graunt it to any person or persons for the terms of 7 yeares, so it be not chargable to the country, or else take it to himselfe & his heires as his owne inheritance for ever, provided it be kept at such a place & at such a price as may be most convenient to the country & pleasinge to the Generall Court."

Thus the Indian trail along the shore and the Massachusetts path inland became the arteries of communication between the two governments, which although separated by only about the same distance as that between the most distant towns of the Bay Colony, had little occasion for intercourse except in connection with the defense against a common enemy,

[1]Ibidem, pages 114 and 127.
[2]Massachusetts Bay records, Vol. III, page 128.

and in religious affairs, until the deposition of Andros resulted in the joining of the two colonies in 1692.

Then, with a mutuality of interest, the erection of a uniform system of government under the Crown, the establishment of large trade relations, courts and a legislature, the necessity for real highways grew. The records of both governments abound with orders for the rebuilding and repairs of the integral parts of the roads which formed this highway, complaints to grand juries of its unsafe condition and laws for its use and against its obstruction.

The legislature of the Bay Colony early realized the importance of a safe road between Plymouth and Boston and its northern towns and the inequality of putting the cost of the bridges upon the towns in which they were located. In 1648, it passed this law:—

"This Court considering that bridges in country highways are for the benefit of the country in general and that it may be unequal to lay the charge thereof on particular towns Doth order that they shall be built by the Magistrates who are likewise empowered to issue out warrants to the constable to impress such workmen in the township as shall be needful to secure and repair the same."

An additional reason for the statute, especially that part relating to the impressment of workmen, existed in the fact that towns and particular officers charged with keeping highways and bridges in repair, "many times cannot procure workmen to do the same."

One of the most frequent travellers upon the Boston-Plymouth road was Judge Samuel Sewall, a member of the Superior Court of Judicature for many years from 1692, and a conscientious, if prolix, diarist.

In travelling upon horseback between his home in Boston and his judicial duties at Plymouth he used both the Country Way through Scituate and Marshfield and the Queen Anne Turnpike.

His habit, as shown in the pages of his diary, was to journey to the house of Capt. John Mill in Braintree, where he would bait his horse; thence to "Brigadier Cushin's Tavern" which stood just off the highway in the direction of Cushing's pond in Hingham, where he would dine; and bearing southeast from Accord pond, continue his journey to Barstow's tavern kept by the son of that William Barstow's who built the bridge over the North River and was "allowed to draw and sell wine beer and strong waters" to the "passengers or others that shall have occasion."

Judge Sewall was usually met here by under sheriff Thomas Bryant[1] and by him accompanied to Plymouth. Frequently the High Sheriff himself came out of Plymouth, met him up the road and escorted him into town. Here is the entry made in the year 1704 of one of those journeys:—

"March 25. Col. Hathorne and I travel to Braintry * * * * Bait at Cushings. He shows me Accord Pond hardly a quarter of a mile out of the rods. Dine at Barkers[2] in company with Major Eels, his son, Mr. Stoddard, Dr. Samsons and others. Sheriff Warren meets us there; before we got away Major Walley and Leverett[3] come in. We got to Plimo. ½ hour before Sun set. March 29th. Adjourned sine die before Noon. Dined and got to Cushings about Sun-set. In the evening Mr. Cushing desired me to pray which I did, and sang the staves of the 137 Psalm omitting Edom. Mr. Cushing told us Mr. Danforth[4] used to sing. I showed Mr. Leverett Accord Pond as came along."

Four years later Judge Sewall records another journey to Plymouth. The judges invariably travelled together and were not infrequently accompanied by the lawyers who had business before the court which the former were to hold. On this occasion he was accompanied by his associate John Hathorne and by Jonathan Corwin a leading lawyer. All of these gentlemen had, twelve years before, been members of the Special Court which had been convened at Salem for the trial of the witches, all had been very active as magistrates in their prosecution and as Sewall had

[1]Father of Rev. Lemuel Bryant of Quincy and ancestor of Gridley Bryant who built the Quincy Granite Railway.
[2]In Pembroke.
[3]John Walley and John Leverett were two other members of the Court.
[4]Thomas Danforth, one of the first judges of the Superior Court of Judicature of the Province. He died in 1699.

at that time recanted[1] his opinion on witchcraft, the others with the exception of Stoughton very generally agreeing with him, it may be assumed that their discourse on this journey was not upon that subject. In fact he was taking his fellow travellers a little out of their way in order to meet a dear friend[2] a non-believer in witchcraft, who lived on the banks of the North River a short distance from Barstows.

This is the record:—

"March 26, 1708. Col. Hathorne, Mr. Corwin, Mr. Taft and I set out for Plimouth, get to Job Randall's about Sunsetting. March 27th. Mr. Eels preached in the Forenoon; Mr. Taft in the afternoon; sup. at Mr. Eels. March 28. Set out for Plimouth. Got there before any stress of rain. Mr. Dudley and Cook came in very wet March 30. I go into the Meeting House. Mar. 31. Col. Church goes (from Plymouth) with us. p. m. Between Jone's River and the old Rode my Horse falls; yet I fall not off; neither had I any hurt. Lodge at Barrstos. April 1. Breakfast at Cushings. Got home well about 3 p. m. Laus Deo."

Judge Sewall and his associates did not always travel on the way that led by Barstow's and Barkers'. In

[1]There was a custom in the churches at this time, upon the occasion of sad or joyful happenings to a person, his family or most intimate friends to "put up a Bill" to be read from the pulpit while the proponent arose and stood in his place during the reading. Such petitions and confessions were also offered by wrong-doers and penitents. On this occasion, Judge Sewall having seen the true light, regretting sincerely the part which he judicially took as a member of the Special Court in the Witchcraft persecutions, and wishing to publicly announce not only his fault but his contrition, put up this "Bill" on Fast Day May 22, 1697, at the South Church, standing while it was being read, "in view of the whole Assembly."

"Samuel Sewall, sensible of the reiterated strokes of God upon himself and family; and being sensible, that as to the Guilt contracted upon the opening of the late Commission of Oyer and Terminer at Salem (to which the order for this day relates) he is, upon many accounts, more concerned than any that he knows of, Desires to take the blame and shame of it, Asking pardon of men and especially desiring prayers that God, who has an unlimited Authority, would pardon that sin and all other his sins; personal and relative; and according to his infinite Benignity and Sovereignty, Not Visit the sin of him, or of any other upon himself or any of his, nor upon the Land; But that he would powerfully defend him against all Temptations to Sin, for the future; and vouchsafe him the efficacious, saving Conduct of his Word and Spirit."

It is tradition that Lieut. Governor Stoughton who presided at the trials, had no such feeling concerning the action of the special tribunal. When informed of Sewall's action he is reputed to have said that he "had no such confession to make as he had acted according to the best light which Faith had given" him. The Diary of Samuel Sewall, Mass. Hist. Soc. Coll. Fifth Series, Vol. I., Page 443.

[2]Rev. Nathaniel Eels.

12

Rev. Nathaniel Eels, pastor of the Second Church at Scituate, he had a warm friend to whose preaching he delighted to listen. Other friends in Scituate and Marshfield were John Cushing, who succeeded him on the Superior Court upon his resignation, and Nathaniel Thomas, his contemporary upon the bench for six years. To visit these latter men he often went to Plymouth, by way of Scituate and Marshfield, traversing "the Country Way." On March 25, 1700:—

"Set out with Mr. Cooke for Plimouth, visited Mr. Torrey, staid near 3 hours, then to Mr. Morton's where Maj. Gen· Winthrop[1] came to us late, so got late to Scituate to Mr. Cushings lodg'd there just by the ruins of Mr. Chauncey's[2] house. Maj. General had appointed to visit said Cushing. Were so belated that failed Major Thomas, who with some other Gentlemen waited for us at the old Ferry on Marshfield side.

Tuesday, March 26. The wind is very bleak that it was ready to put me into an Ague, having rid late the night before. Had a noble treat at Maj. Thomas's. Mr. Sheriff and Gentlemen were so wearied that they were afraid of some Miscarriage at the Ferry."

Nor was this journey always made entirely on horseback. In 1716, Judge Sewall tells in his diary of a trip by way of the shore towns to attend Court in Plymouth thus:—

"March 24. I set out for Scituate with Judge Lynde, dine at Capt. Mill's, bait at little Hingham[3]. Lodge at Mr. Jenkyns[4] by the Sea-side in Scituate. Hear Mr. Pitcher[5] who dwells on the land where Mr. Chauncey dwelt. Sup'd at his house. He is much recovered of a dangerous sickness. Gave him a Psalm-book, one of Dr. Cotton Mather's Sermons with a crown for contribution. Psalm-Book covered with Turkey-Leather.

March 26. Mr. Turner, and the Sheriffs Deputy, Briant, conducted us by way of the New Ferry settled at the Mouth of

[1]Waite Winthrop. Chief Justice of the Superior Court of Judicature of the Province.
[2]Rev. Charles Chauncey, a former minister at Scituate and second President of Harvard College.
[3]Cohasset.
[4]Thomas Jenkins. His father, Edward, was licensed to keep an 'ordinary' at Scituate in 1677. It stood at the corner of Kent Street and Central Street, where Satuit Brook flows into the harbor.
[5]Rev. Nathaniel Pitcher, pastor of the first church and a son-in-law of Sewall's friend, Judge John Cushing.

the North River.[1] Bait at the Ferry-house in the Marshfield side. From thence to Cook's. After Diner I rode with Mr. Justice Thomas in his Calash to Town (Plymouth). Gave the sheriff and his Attendants a Dux. of Dr. Incr. Mather's Sermons concerning Christ the Great Saviour."

Finally as the roads became better adapted to the use of vehicles, travel in calashes and coaches was more general. Two years before Judge Sewall left the bench he used the latter:—

"Monday April 25 (1726). Judge Davenport, Mr. Cooper and I set out for plimouth in Blak's Coach, Ben Swett waiting on us; got thither a little after Sun-set. Lodge at Mr. Cushman's.

Satterday April 30, 11 m. Mr. Dudley returns home. 3 p. m. Mr. Justice Quincy ditto. Sewall, Lynde, Davenport continue to hold the Court till about 6 p.m. and then Adjourn sine die.

2nd day, May 2. Gave Mr. Lenard a 20s. Bill. Mr. Cooper pray'd on Satterday morn. Baited at Bairstow's. Din'd at Hingham; had a noble Treat set before us at Col. Quincy's[2] Got well home before nine. The honored ancient Elder Faunce[3] and Deacon Jacobe of Scituate kindly visited me. Laus Deo.

It was not without much opposition that the condition of the principal highways was bettered at the beginning of the new century which saw the infant Province also just starting into life. One of the first things done was to pass, December 6, 1693-4:—

"An Act for the better Amending and Keeping in Repair and Clear the Highways and Common Roads leading from Town to Town and Place to Place, and for Laying out new Highways and turning old Highways where it shall be Needful."

Under this act surveyors of highways were annually to be chosen from among the freeholders of each town who were to take care of "all highways, private ways, causeways and bridges within their respective towns." They were empowered to "cut down, dig up or remove as well all sorts of trees, bushes, stone fences, rayles, gates, inclosures or other thing or things as may any wayes straighten hurt hinder or incommode the highwayes; as also to dig for stone, gravel, clay, marl,

[1]Little's Bridge.
[2]Judge Edmund Quincy, the grandfather of Josiah Quincy, Jr., who defended Capt. Preston in October 1770 for his participation in the Boston Massacre.
[3]Thomas Faunce an elder of the First Church at Plymouth. He was born in 1647 and lived to the age of ninety-nine years. He was the one living link between the Pilgrims, many of whom he well knew, and succeeding generations.

14

sand or earth in any land not planted or enclosed." They might also impress every male person between the ages of sixteen and sixty for work upon the roads with his "cart or teem," under penalty of two shillings for the cart or team. Twenty-five years later, the penalty was increased to five and ten shillings respectively.

Surveyors so chosen were themselves subject to a forfeiture of twenty shillings for refusal to accept and take the oath of office; and five pounds, if having qualified, they neglected this duty.

On March 7, 1695-6, came an order reviving and confirming an order of the General Court of the Plymouth Colony passed in 1682, respecting the maintenance of the Jone's River and Eel river[1] bridges. The former had recently burned down. It was ordered to be rebuilt. The same order required that Scituate, Marshfield and Duxbury, should maintain North River bridge "according to the former agreement of Plymouth Colony and those towns, and to be free from being charged towards the building of any other bridge out of their respective townships." This was the bridge originally built by William Barstow. It spanned the river about three quarters of a mile below the place where Governor Winthrop crossed it on the back of the man for whom it was named,—Luddam's ford. The present side, very near the bridge of 1656, was occupied in 1710. Little's Bridge, the first crossing North River at a point nearest its mouth, was the last to be built. It was not accomplished until 1825. For two hundred years prior to that time a ferry had been constantly maintained by order of the Colony, Province and State, first by William Vassal, then by Ralph

[1]On the south side of Plymouth town, below Hobshole. The bridge was built in 1648 by the inhabitants of the community called "the Eel River." It benefitted the towns to the southward and in 1649 the Colony Court ordered that the towns of "Yarmouth, Barnstable and Sandwich contribute fifteen pounds in good and current pay unto the inhabitant of the Eel River aforesaid towards the charge by them expended in building the aforesaid bridge * * * * proportionable to their rates in publick charges; * * * or otherwise the said inhabitants to have libertie to comence suit against the towns aforesaid, in respect of the perticular aforesaid, as they shall see reason." Plymouth Colony Records, Vol. II., Page 147.

Chapman and later by Thomas Doggett, of Marshfield, whose name it still bears.

The individual aversion to work upon the highways extended to the towns themselves in building and repairing them. The cause of this slothfulness is not today apparent. There is abundant evidence, nevertheless, that it existed.

In 1726 Amos Turner was the representative to the provincial General Court from Scituate. A way and bridge which had previously been built over Bound Brook[1] by the Conihasset Partners before 1656, was to be "repaired and cleared." Hingham refused to do its part; whereupon the town of Scituate instructed its representative to file with the Council a petition:—

"shewing that there is a difference between the towns of Scituate and Hingham about laying out an highway over Bound Brook River so called; but in regard to said brook is the bounds between the said towns[2] and divides the counties of Plymouth and Suffolk the town of Scituate cannot lay out their highway because the town of Hingham will not joyn with them therein; therefore praying that this Court would appoint and impower a committee to lay out said way and do what they shall think proper to be done in order to settle the same and put an end to the differences between said towns."

An order of notice upon this petition returnable upon "ye second Tuesday of the next May session" was an efficient means to end the quarrel between the two towns. When it was served upon Hingham, she joined with her neighbor and the highway was laid out and built. It followed the line and direction of the road as it is today, marked by a bronze tablet on Bound Rock, a natural monument of the boundry adopted by the forefathers which has stood through the centuries.

This means of communication was called when completed, by the same name given it by the Conihasset Partners—"The Country Way." Local historians have attached the title "The King's Highway" to both

[1]Dean—History of Scituate. Pratt—The Early Planters of Scituate. Bound Brook was the division line between the Plymouth and Massachusetts Bay colonies and under the Provincial government, between the two countries of Suffolk and Plymouth.

[2]Cohasset, then a parish of Hingham, called Little Hingham, was made a township in 1770.

this and parts of the "Massachusetts Path"; but the only King's Highway of the Pilgrims was that which in Plymouth extended to Barnstable and Yarmouth on the south and Namaskeeset (Middleborough) on the northwest[1].

The disaffection at this time over "Court Orders" for the building of highways and bridges which should afford a better opportunity for travel between the various localities in the province was general. This may have been in part due to the enactment which empowered grand juries to indict a municipality for neglect of its highways and bridges, a law of which the provincial freeman, extremely jealous of his rights and privileges frequently availed himself. The town of Dorchester was so indicted in 1750, for failure to keep the "Great Bridge" over Neponset river in repair. The following remonstrance shows the large use to which this bridge was put in travel between Plymouth and Boston, and is a good example as well, of the way in which the then infant "spirit of 76" struck back when attacked:—

"Jany 25, 1751-2[2]. A remonstrance of Capt. Robert Spur[3] and others a committee for the Town of Dorchester setting forth that ye said Town is presented by the Grand Jury for the County of Suffolk to the Court of General Sessions of the Peace for the said County now held at Boston, for their not keeping in Repair the Great Bridge over Neponset River and for as much as the said Bridge never was accounted to belong to the town of Dorchester to repair, the Inhabitants not having near so much benefit as many other Towns in this and other Counties, & the said Town cannot have an Impartial Trial, both Justices and Juries being Parties in the case & therefore praying that this Court would provide Relief for the said Town & in the meantime stop prosecution."

This contention that the town could not get a fair trial because both bench and jury were parties interested was both ingenious and forceful; but it was not

[1] Davis—Ancient Landmarks of Plymouth. Map at page 161.
[2] Province Laws, Vol. III, 1742-1756.
[3] He was that Dorchester representative who in 1754 uncompromisingly and persistently refused to join in the recommendation of the Albany Congress that the Colonies unite against French aggressions. He boldly led the majority.

good law. It apparently however had its effect upon the body addressed, for on June 3, 1752-3, it was:—

"Ordered—that the Petition and the Answer thereto be revived; and the matter being fully considered, Resolved the Bridge over Neponset River referred to in the Petition, is and ought to be accounted a County Bridge; and the Justices of the County of Suffolk are hereby ordered to take effectual care that said Bridge be forthwith put into good Repair accordingly."

An Act of the Legislature passed June 18, 1794, required maps of all the towns of the new Commonwealth to be prepared by actual surveys showing the location of all country ways leading from place of place and town to town, therein and filed with the Secretary,[1] The means is thus afforded of exactly locating the highways between Plymouth and Boston as they existed in the early days of Massachusetts following the Revolution. Indeed the ways thus depicted follow very nearly the "Country Way" of the coast line towns and the "Massachusetts Path" over which Winthrop rode in 1632, both of which are accurately identified by ancient landmarks and monuments which are still extant.

The only break in the continuity of the "Country Way" on these maps occurs in that of Marshfield. The estimable engineer who made the survey and who modestly witholds his name therefrom, having in mind the provision of the law that all roads which were direct means of communication between adjacent towns should be depicted thereon, makes this memorandum:-

"The reason why no Road is delineated, is because by Reason of the locality of the Town there is no Highway in it that can with propriety deserve the Appellation of a County Road;"

This statement seems to have gone unchallenged. The principal thoroughfare of Marshfield in those days was a waterway—the North River—upon whose banks sturdy Scituate and Marshfield men built, officered and manned the deep sea ships which sailed to India and China, to the West Coast and to Jamaica.

[1]Massachusetts Archives—Town Maps, Vols., 1, 2, 5, 8, 9, 10, 11, 12, and 13.

Travellers on these roads today as they journey through the territory of the Pilgrim and Puritan founders of the Commonwealth will pass the sites of the early homes of many of both. They may visit that of Governor Bradford, in Kingston; Caresrull, the seat of Governor Winslow, of Marshfield; and may enter the house now standing on the same acres and built by his grandson, Isaac Winslow, Judge of Probate and Colonel of Provincial militia. They may climb the hill in Duxbury, owned by Captain Myles Standish, and from beneath the shadow of his statue listen to the booming of the same sea that was at once his welcome and his requiem. They can visit the homestead which John Alden left to a proud and numerous progeny, and in Marshfield again, stand where Webster upon his homecoming in 1852, said to his neighbors; It is:

"the fact that you among whom I have so long lived and dwelt, and who know me so well, have manifested such esteem, that calls forthwith my gratitude; and I pour out to you friends and neighbors, on my part from the bottom of my heart, the feelings of mutual and reciprocal regard and friendship."

When the North river has been crossed at Doggett's ferry, the farm of William Cushing, Chief Justice of the Supreme Court of Judicature of Massachusetts and Justice of the Supreme Court of the United States, appears at Belle House Neck. Nearby is his burial place surrounded with a granite wall. Protected within the enclosure is the modest shaft of the same material bearing the single word "Cushing." It is tradition that his widow, between whom and himself there was great disparity of years but strong attachment and intense affection, and whose marriage to the justice was opposed by his family, was denied the right of sepulture beside her husband. It is the fact that her body lies buried in another cemetery.

A quarter of a mile further north is the scene of the massacre at the Block House on the First Herring Brook, in King Phillip's War; and near by the mill on the same stream built by John Stockbridge in 1640,—

the mill of Wordsworth's poem, the Old Oaken Bucket. As the highway rises over Brushy Hill in Scituate, it passes through the homestead farm of Nicholas Wade where he kept the "ordinary" in 1657, and where his descendant in the ninth generation now resides. This record for devotion to the ancestral acres is duplicated a mile farther on where the progeny of Capt. Michael Peirce, the Indian fighter, cultivate and dwell upon the land which he first purchased in the Conihasset tract in 1647.

Across Bound Brook into Cohasset there spreads to the east and south the "meadowe grounds," for the ownership of which Hingham and Scituate stoutly contended for a quarter of a century. In this controversy Governor Bradford, Edward Winslow, his son Josiah, Timothy Hatherly, Nathaniel Tilden, Capt. Thomas Southworth and Cornet Robert Stetson, for the Plymouth Colony, and John Endicott, Israel Stoughton, William Aspinwall, Joseph Andrews, Capt. Ebenezer Lusher, Roger Clap of Dorchester, and Joseph Fisher, for the Bay Colony, from time to time pugnaciously put forth their respective claims to the territory. The zeal of the latter in the controversy led them at one time to the extent of claiming that Bound Brook was in reality the Charles river, which as they subsequently found "would fetch in Scituate and more."[1]

On, through Hingham, both ancient road and modern highway, pass the "Old Ship" where General Benjamin Lincoln and all the early generations of Thaxters, Cushings, Jacobs, and other stalwart Puritan families worshipped God after their own nonconformist fashion and chanted the quaint hymns of Sternhold and Hopkins as the stanzas were deaconed off to them, line by line.

If, in leaving Plymouth these same travelers shall choose the way following the line of the old "Massaachusetts Path" of colony days and the "Queen Anne

[1] Winthrop, page 283.

Turnpike" of the province, they will pass in Kingston the site of the homestead of Governor Bradford; in Pembroke the now decaying meeting house of the Friends, and cross the present bridge over North River only a short distance to the eastward from where the first bridge spanning that stream was built by Barstow. They will see to the right, along both banks of the river the locations of the shipyards of the Briggs, the Turners, the Quaker Wantons and the descendants of him who built that first bridge. Five miles further on they may be shown Accord Pond as it was shown to Judge Leverett by his associate Sewall. If the traveller is an inquisitive one and seeks to know the derivation of the name given to this attractive sheet of water he will be told that when the commissioners from the two colonies were disputing over the boundary line between the two patents, they were in accord as to the pond being a monument of that boundary; or that it was the northeast corner boundary of the land that had been awarded Timothy Hatherly in "accord and satisfaction" of his demand for more land in Scituate."[1]

The Weymouth Back River was in the early days as now the boundary between that town and Hingham. It was reached after leaving the "Old Ship" by a detour to the west and north, by what is now the United States Naval Magazine. On its banks in 1793, was Rice's Mill and nearby Rice's tavern.

Crossing the Weymouth Fore River and through Quincy to the "Stone Church," the traveller to Boston in 1783 found the road at that point bearing to the south and west by the "Vice Presidents house" of John Adams and near, over against Dorchester, the home of Capt. Hull. In Dorchester the same highway would lead him by the mansion of James Swan, the friend of Lafayette and neighbor of General Henry Knox, so stubborn and devoted an adherent to a principle, that he suffered imprisonment in a French prison for twenty-two years rather than pay a demand unjustly

[1]Pratt—the Early Planters of Scituate.

21

made and framed into a judgment for debt. Here also he would tread the way first laid out by Roger Clap, Selectman, the ancestor of the Reverend Thomas Clapp of Scituate, who was "rector of the College at New Haven" in 1740, its champion before an hostile legislature and the real builder of Yale College.

Stoughton, Clapp, Leverett, Bradford, Winslow, Standish, Alden, Hatherly, Dudley, Leverett, Adams, Lincoln, Cushing and Quincy; with all of these pioneers and patriots and more, are these ways and their landmarks in one way and another associated.

As they grew from mere paths of the wilderness to country highways and macadamized modern arteries of travel, they have marked the growth of municipality, commonwealth and nation. They have been real pathways of bravery, ambition, high purpose and devotion.

[1]Before this date a road had been built leading from Hingham at Liberty Plain through Weymouth, by Arnold's Tavern and across the Monatiquot River to Quincy, where it joined the road above described.